ALCRAFT, Rob

A visit to Germany

A Visit to
GERMANY

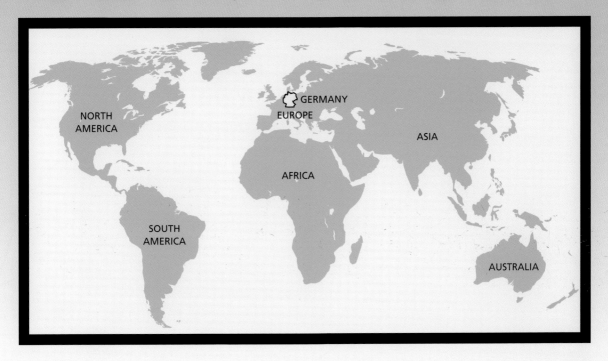

Rob Alcraft

Heinemann
LIBRARY

First published in Great Britain by Heinemann Library,
Halley Court, Jordan Hill, Oxford OX2 8EJ
a division of Reed Educational and Professional Publishing Ltd.

Heinemann is a registered trademark of Reed Educational & Professional Publishing Ltd.

OXFORD   MELBOURNE   AUCKLAND
JOHANNESBURG   BLANTYRE   GABORONE
IBADAN   PORTSMOUTH (NH) USA   CHICAGO

Designed by AMR
Illustrations by Art Construction
Printed in Hong Kong/China

03 02 01 00 99
10 9 8 7 6 5 4 3 2 1

ISBN 0 431 08331 2

British Library Cataloguing in Publication Data

Alcraft, Rob, 1966–
  A visit to Germany
  1.Germany – Juvenile literature
  I.Title II.Germany
  943

Acknowledgements
The Publishers would like to thank the following for permission to reproduce photographs:
AKG Photo, p. 29; J Allan Cash, pp. 10, 17, 19, 28; Robert Harding Picture Library, pp. 21, 22, 27; (G Hellier) p. 7; (Larsen-Collinge) p. 13; Spectrum Colour Library, p. 24; Stock Market, (John Henley) p. 25; Telegraph Colour Library, pp. 6, 27; (Werner Otto) pp. 5, 9, 14; (Bildarchiv Huber) p. 8; (David Noton) pp. 11, 26; (Josef Beck) p. 15; (Antonio Mo) p. 16; (Pfeiffer) p. 18; Trevor Clifford, p.12; Trip, (M O'Brien) p. 20; (M Barlow) p. 23.

Cover photograph reproduced with permission of Britstock – IFA/Oertel

Every effort has been made to contact copyright holders of any material reproduced in this book. Any omissions will be rectified in subsequent printings if notice is given to the Publisher.

Any words appearing in bold, **like this**, are explained in the Glossary.

Contents

Germany

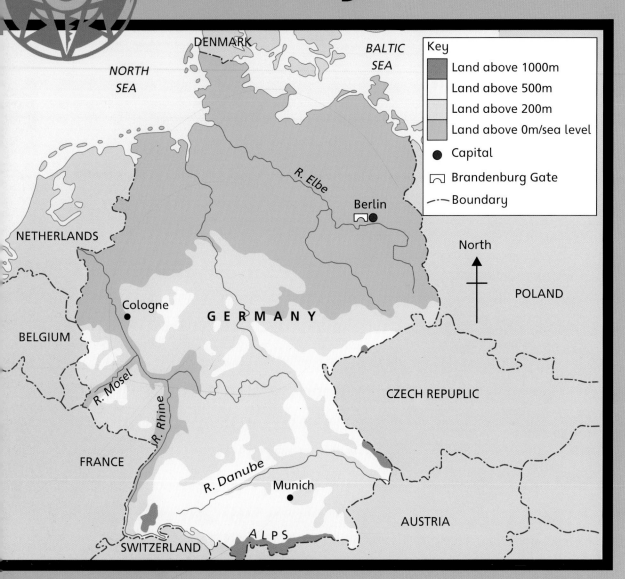

Germany is a big country. It is in the middle of Europe.

There are many big cities in Germany, like Berlin and Cologne (above). Most people in Germany live in cities.

Land

In the north of Germany the land is flat
and low. There are **marshes**, and islands in
the sea. Here the weather is wet and mild.

6

In the south of Germany are forests, **meadows** and mountains. The mountains are called the Alps. Winters here are very cold with lots of snow.

Landmarks

Germany's biggest river is the Rhine. It is 1320 kilometres long. Along the river banks are **vineyards**, and beautiful castles.

This is the Brandenburg Gate. It is
200 years old, and stands in the middle
of Berlin. Berlin is Germany's **capital** city.

Homes

Germany's towns and cities are crowded and busy. There is not much space for big houses and gardens. Most people live in flats.

In the countryside there are old farm houses. They are built from wood. They have wide **sloping** roofs so the snow will slide off.

Food

In Germany lunch is the biggest meal.
There might be **schnitzel** with mashed
potatoes and vegetables.

Sausage called wurst is a special German food. There are over 200 different kinds. Some are eaten hot, and some are eaten cold, some are sliced, some are **spicy**.

Clothes

Germans wear **modern** clothes, like jeans and T-shirts. In cold winters people have to wrap up warm in thick coats and boots.

At parties and festivals many Germans wear special clothes. They might wear leather shorts called lederhosen, and a cap with feathers like this boy.

Work

Many Germans have jobs in factories, offices and shops. They make cars, lorries, machines and **electrical goods**.

In the country, farmers keep cows and pigs.
They also grow grain, potatoes and fruit.
The weather and soil are good for farming.

Transport

Germans like driving. There are many big **motorways**. There are train stations in every city, and busy airports.

On Germany's rivers and **canals** ships and **barges** carry coal, steel and oil. On the River Rhine ships from the sea can travel right into Germany.

language

In Germany people speak German.
Some German and English words sound
nearly the same, like 'buch' and 'book',
and 'haus' and 'house'.

In German there are two ways of speaking. One way you must use with adults and important people. The other way is for friends.

School

School starts early in Germany, at 7.30am. There is school on a Saturday too. But lessons always finish at lunchtime, and everyone has the afternoon off.

The children in this picture are going on a school trip to the zoo. When they are in class they learn maths and German. They also have English lessons.

Free time

Many Germans like going on holidays. In the summer, families often go to the beach. In winter when it snows, some people go skiing in the Alps.

Many Germans love sport. They join
sports clubs, and play tennis and
football. They go walking and camping
in the forests and mountains.

Celebrations

Christmas is the most important celebration in Germany. There are special markets and funfairs.
The streets sparkle with lights.

Every year in July there is a children's festival. Children dress up in costumes and parade through the streets.

The Arts

Germany is famous for its beautiful music. Beethoven and Schumann were German. They wrote music for **orchestras,** and for the piano.

Have you heard the story of Sleeping Beauty? This is a very old German **fairy tale**, written down by two brothers called Grimm.

Factfile

Name	The Federal Republic of Germany
Capital	Germany's **capital** city is called Berlin.
Language	German
Population	There are 80 million people living in Germany.
Money	German money is called marks.
Religion	Most Germans are Christians but there are many other religions too.
Products	Germany makes chemicals, cars and lorries, machines, **electrical goods**.

Words you can learn

guten Tag (goo-ten targ)	hello
Auf Wiedersehen (owf vee-d-say-n)	goodbye
ja (ya)	yes
nein (nine)	no
danke schön (danke shern)	thank you
bitte (bitter)	please
ein (eye-n)	one
zwei (svi)	two
drei (dry)	three

Glossary

barge	a boat with a flat bottom. It can float in shallow water.
canal	a river dug by people
capital	the city where the government is based
electrical goods	things like televisions and videos which use electricity
fairy tale	a story where anything can happen
marsh	a flat, wet place
meadow	grassy land
modern	new, up-to-date
motorway	a big, fast road. Often they have three lanes of cars going each way.
orchestra	a group of people who play music
schnitzel	fried meat in breadcrumbs
slope	lean
spicy	food with a strong, hot taste
vineyard	place where grapes are grown

Index